SCRATCH TO A MILLION

By Dean Thistleton

My story of how to create a business from
nothing and build a million pound turnover

Edited and compiled by KRD Agency – www.krdagency.com

TABLE OF CONTENTS

Dean Thistleton is the Founder and CEO of Concept Pools Group. Within the successful group structure are several companies: Concept Pools, The Swimming Pool Shop, Tanqua Pools, The Swim Club and DAT Ventures. Dean is a very focused, driven and passionate entrepreneur who takes great pleasure in helping other entrepreneurs succeed; in their businesses, through the Renegade process.

Dean currently lives on a farm set in the Huddersfield countryside in Yorkshire, together with Lauren with whom he has beautiful twin girls Ellie and Grace, and two dogs Mia and Kia. His hobbies are working out in the gym and mixed martial arts training as well as being a huge advocate for personal growth and development.

Deans' advice to any business owner is:

"Be the best version of you. Be clear on your goals and visions and take control of and design a life that suits you. Work hard to find financial freedom and live life on your terms then help others to do the same."

Wise words indeed.

FOREWARD

Being in business is a lonely old place at times.

For many, the transition from employee to employer is not an easy one, after all there is no "boss" making sure you turn up on time, with the right gear, and to do the job you are getting paid to do. It's all down to you, your values, your work ethic, and self-discipline and self-motivation.

I think, secretly, everyone would love to run their own business. They fall in love with the idea of being their own boss. Late starts, early finishes, better holidays, more time with the family, bigger house, faster car and obviously, more money. The fact is, running your own business invariably starts with the exact opposite.

You work longer and harder than ever before, you are in before the sun rises and come home after it's gone down.

You make way less money at the outset. You have a choice - pay the bills to keep the doors open, or pay yourself. Tough choice to make.

The family takes a back seat and those long, stress free, sleepy, lazy holidays are out of the question.

The house is the same as before, but now you've used it to guarantee your borrowing - so now it's all on the line. You could lose it all with one bad deal or wrong call.

As for the car, it's probably the businesses van or the cheapest thing you could find on a lease.

That's the normal reality for most when they set out as a business owner; it seems fashionable now to say "I am an entrepreneur!"

There is a stat that we hear all the time, 8 out of 10 businesses fail in the 5 years.

If you get past those 5 you should be home and dry, right? Wrong.

For those that get into and beyond that, then 80% of those also fail between year 5 and 10.

The odds are stacked against you, and that is why this book is all about pulling back some control and lessening those odds.

I first met Dean (Rhino as I like to call him!) in 2016.

I had taken the plunge, as had he, to join a Mastermind group.

That sounds very grandiose, and perhaps I should outline what that is.

Dean talks about this and his experience later in this book, so I won't steal too much of his thunder. In life and business it is all about learning and developing and, like Dean, I have a passion for being the best version of myself I can possibly be. For many years I read books, listened to podcasts and attended the odd event held by some internet sensation. I was always thirsty to keep getting better. Then I started taking myself seriously and found a great coach and enrolled in my first mastermind.

A proper mastermind group (there are loads of imitations out there, so be careful) pitches 8-10 business owners in a room where they get to discuss their challenges and opportunities to each other. The time in the "hot seat" is, quite frankly, priceless, but for any small business owner it's a big investment in time and cash.

As we sat there on day one, nervously looking around the room, firstly to work out why we were doing this and questioning our sanity, but mainly out of concern that we would have nothing to offer the other eight business owners in the room.

I immediately knew I would get on with Dean. He had an aura about him. It was like he had a purpose, a mission, and this was the place that would take him and his business to the next level.

I just watched, in awe, as he took in all the advice, but then returned back to Huddersfield and did what most simply fail to do.

Action and Implementation.

He actually did what he said he was going to do.

From day one, I have never heard Dean make an excuse.

He has never failed to take action and complete his accountabilities that we all give each other at the end of every hot seat session we have.

On that first day, my business was 3 times the size of Dean's, I employed 13 staff across 2 countries, and I was in the process of exiting. My life had lost its purpose, my mojo had gone, as he so nicely put it.

It is fair to say we have both watched each other on our respective journeys.

I still meet up with Dean for our Mastermind groups every quarter and I have marvelled at his adventure to date. We invariably talk for hours about life and business over a small glass or two of "Pinot for Deano," as he is tells me how he plans for world domination!

His business is now 4 times the size of mine when I exited, his year on year growth, which in itself is so hard to manage, has been unbelievable.

Dean isn't one of these internet guru's that tells you exactly what you should be doing but have never done it themselves.

These days the world seems full of 21 year-old life and business coaches that seem to spend all their time in Ferrari's or sitting on beaches and will sell you the secret of their success.

I know for a fact, Dean has lived into this book. He has done everything that he is telling you that you should do. You would be well placed to follow his steps and give yourself a better chance of not being one of the 8 out of 10.

This book isn't a fluffy "How To" guide that will guarantee you riches and an easy life. It's Dean's recipe for success in business in one small book.

The graft, the persistence, the discipline is all in here.

How he gets help from others and how he has his own coach and mastermind experience.

The practicalities, the necessities and the 'nice to have' are all in here and if you are reading this, then it goes without saying, you already have the mindset to learn and get better.

We all have a plan or an idea, but what many of us fail to do is what Dean does best – Act.

A plan or an idea without action and implementation is just a dream, and Dean would tell you in his broad northern accent, "Dreams are like the Tooth Fairy – they're just not real."

He implements his own motto to get things done, just like he did with this book - and why you are able to benefit from him, his advice and his journey in the rest of this book..

JFDI – Just f***ing do it!!

Steve Matthews

Entrepreneur, Business Owner (Failed and Succeeded), Husband, Father, Life Lover, Red Wine Drinker, Trier.

INTRODUCTION

Over the following pages, I'll be sharing my journey of how I started my businesses from scratch. When I say scratch, I literally mean starting from nothing. I'll show you how I took a desire to run my own business and built it from zero, to a million-pound turnover.

I'll share with you everything I've learned and executed in my companies to help assist you on your journey. These are not secrets alone; they are the ups and downs of growing and scaling a business. Don't get me wrong, I'm not claiming to be an expert and I'm still learning every day myself, but I'm well into my journey and that's what I want to share with you, to help you to grow, build and develop a successful business. These experiences have cost me financially and emotionally as well as my time, but it's an investment that has been worthwhile.

When I started my first business my aspirations were to reach a turnover of 1 million pounds. A few years in and I'm thankful to have achieved this goal, and more, and I'm looking forward to sharing how I did that with all you entrepreneurs. The aim of my little book is to provide sound and solid advice to both existing businesses and new start-ups, and wherever you are on your business journey, I've included along the way short '*golden nuggets*' and '*advice with value*' that I hope you can take and put into practice for yourself. You'll also find space to write your own notes, so do take time to scribble down those thoughts that pop into your head as you read through.

If you've decided it's time to move on from existing in your current job, to a position of owning your own business, or if you've decided to follow your dreams and build your own business in hope of finding financial freedom, my hat goes off to you, because you're a doer and you're chasing your dreams.

Good luck.

CHAPTER 1   PLANNING

FAIL TO PLAN, PLAN TO FAIL

Owning your own business will no doubt be a challenge at times and I'm sure you didn't come to this decision lightly. If you have the time and energy to make this a success, then you're up for the challenge. You will need to prepare for the journey ahead and business is exactly that, a journey. It's important though, right from the get-go to always keep in your mind, 'the journey needs to be enjoyed'. It should not drain away your energy, your family or your life.

How you plan your journey at the start is the most important task you need to work on, before you do anything else.

Planning your journey will consist of:

- goals
- short term visions
- long term visions… to name just a few.

When most budding entrepreneurs begin to think about setting up their business, they tend to neglect any form of goal setting or visioning.

It's a good idea to maybe start with the end game in mind. For example, what do you want to achieve from the business? Is it financial growth and security? Are you building the business to sell or simply to pass down to a family member once you retire? Do you want to shake things up within your industry such as developing a new product or entering a new market? Whatever your reason(s) you must know your end game and then join the dots back to the start. Having no end game is like setting off on a journey in a car with no destination (and no fuel!). The goals, visions and milestones are the satnav for your business, guiding you to your end destination.

There are plenty of resources available to help you with goals and visioning (internet, books, business support groups, etc), but for now I will dive into the first strategic step of how to develop a successful business.

THE BUSINESS PLAN

First you need to start with a **business plan**. This gives an outline of your business, the market in which you'll operate and how it aims to make money.

Can you answer this question?

Why will your business succeed when so many others fail?

Did you know that 9 out of 10 businesses fail in the first 5 years? Whilst I'm sure there are a million and one reasons why they fail I bet a lot could be avoided if a robust business plan was in place. We're not talking a 50-page booklet, just the main essentials will do.

GOLDEN NUGGET

- Be concise.

    It's important that potential investors can understand what your business is all about from a quick glance at your plan. Use simple language throughout and write in short paragraphs.

- Give a summary of your business.

    Make sure you include a summary of your business, sometimes referred to as an "executive summary" and how it will make money right from the start. Drill down into how you will deliver your plan. If financial borrowings are a major part of getting your business off the ground, include brief details of what they are.

A big part of knowing whether your business will be successful is the ability to understand your audience and demographic. The foundations to any successful business will always be, research, research and research.

Spending a little time conducting research will ensure you are clear about your target market, which in turn will help you plan.

You need to know:

- who will you be selling to
- how many other companies are already selling related products
- will your customer base be business to business (B2B); or
- will it be business to customer (B2C) or maybe both,

You may need to differentiate the above points in your plan, so make sure you know your product (or service) and do your research to understand the market place you are looking to enter. Know your competitors, know your audience and know your stuff.

Understanding the finances and numbers is also a pretty critical factor. If your business goal is to make a profit and you can't understand the numbers – you ain't gonna make any money. You need to be very clear on how you will make money and where the profit will be gained (or lost).

A good business plan will serve you well. It will be vital when it comes to securing loans and investment, but it will also serve as a personal tool to help you understand your objectives. There are thousands of business plan templates available on the internet as well as books to assist you in creating a strong robust plan. Find something that suits you and you can develop over time. As your business grows, update your plan. It should be a living and breathing document, so don't just stick in a drawer and forget about it.

As a basic list to get you off the ground, you should be looking to include the following in a business plan:

1. Name, address and contact details: Include the status of your business (eg: Ltd company or sole trader).

2. Contents page: This allows the reader to quickly find anything they are interested in learning more about and may also help you in planning your document, to keep things in an order.

3. An executive summary: This will define, in a nutshell, what your business is and how you plan to operate. It should detail key points and ideally this should be the final part of your plan that you write – but it should be placed at the beginning of the document.

4. Your business and its product or service: Explain what your business will do. How is it different to anything else that is available? If you've done your market research, you should be able to put together a piece that clearly explains why there is a need for your business.

5. The marketplace: Describe what the current marketplace is for your business. Are you a local, national or international business? Are there opportunities that exist in these areas? Don't forget to include thinking about both online and off-line sales opportunities. A SWOT analysis (strengths, weaknesses, opportunities and threats) will be a useful exercise to undertake in helping you understand your marketplace and the environment in which you operate.

6. Marketing and sales: Whilst these two functions are closely interlinked, make sure you know the difference. Putting it simply, marketing is about creating the desire for your product or service and sales is any part of the process or activity that turns that desire into a sale. For example you may need to employ a salesman/team to handle enquiries that your marketing efforts create. Some sales may be quick

to convert whilst other opportunities may need nurturing before they convert. In particular, this is an area that will adapt and grow as your business develops.

7. Management and employees: Who will actually work in and on your business? Do you need a team of people or are you a sole operator? Again, this is likely to be a changing area as your business develops. Think about your structure though and the key personnel that you will need to get your business of the ground and running through its early days.

8. Plant and premises: Where will you be trading from? Include details of what equipment you are going to need and where you are going to be trading from. Remember to have considered costs and allow for this in your financial forecasts and estimates.

9. Financing the business: How is your business and everything in it going to be financed? Will be you starting out with personal savings, or borrowing from friends and family or professional lenders? Make sure you forecast costs as well as projected income, and don't forget to factor in any loan repayments that may need to be made.

Okay, we have the business plan and you're ready to hit the ground running. How do you know your business plan is strong and robust? Has anyone with any business experience looked over and challenged your plan? Most people will probably answer 'no' to those questions. The fact is they don't know anyone who can help them. If you're a self-aware entrepreneur, you'll know that you cannot easily get this advice off the street or from family members. If you're a serious business owner, then actively participating in a growth environment like 729 Renegades enables you to ask questions of the faculty and its members in order to stretch your thinking and gain insight into your business plan, from others that have gone through the same pain points.

DEFINE AND GROW

Out of this chapter, here is your space to clarify your thinking, set your goals, chart the benefits, and hold yourself accountable in order to see your business and personal growth in action.

ACTION NEEDED	BENEFIT TO BUSINESS	IMPLEMENT BY (date)
1		__ / __ / __
2		__ / __ / __
3		__ / __ / __

NOTES

CHAPTER 2 SACRIFICE, COMMITMENT & DECISIONS

When we decide to take the plunge and set up and establish a business, not only have we made a decision, but we've made our first commitment; a commitment to ourselves, our families and to those we may employ. To work hard and be the best we can be and differentiate ourselves from other businesses.

SACRIFICE

If you're a start-up, or even a 20-year established business, ask yourself this question…

"How committed am I to achieving goals and visions for both my business and personal life?"

Don't just give it a quick thought and move on. Dig deep and think about the question. What answer do you get? Do you really show up every day in the best way you can in both your business and personal life?

When I first set up Concept Pools, I was in an 8-year relationship with my girlfriend at the time. My commitment to my company was far more than it was to our relationship apparently (but I disagree for obvious reasons). She didn't approve of me working long hours and weekends to get the company off the ground and fulfil the commitment I promised myself when I first started. I felt I was being held back. I had goals and visions that just didn't align with hers. I'm a risk taker, a go getter and she was a play it safe type of girl. So, I had to decide to sacrifice and end our relationship and go our separate ways.

Once the decision was made, I quickly moved on to find a new house and settle in, so the disruption to my business was minimal. Working from the back bedroom where I had established my office, where I was free to work the hours I needed to grow my business.

Two months of focusing and working hard paid off and I was soon able to take on my first engineer. This was a goal achieved for me, because this freed up my time to work *on* the business, rather than *in* the business. Unfortunately, my time wasn't being spent wisely and I got distracted and took my eye off the ball for a short while with quite a bit of socialising. But, with one thing and another, I began to focus on my business once again.

I had to make a decision and sacrifice the nights out as I was chasing my dream. Once again, I was making a commitment to myself to give everything to scaling my business. So much so, that I moved out of the area and away from friends and family to a farm house in the countryside, where there were no distractions and I could focus on the business.

At the farm I designed my life to suit the needs of growing my business and building a quality lifestyle to support my goals. I converted the stand-alone stables into offices and a meeting room and built a workshop and warehouse. Business was booming and we were scaling year on year, however I was miles out of my comfort zone; managing projects, staff, and finances. In reality I was still an apprentice entrepreneur with an expanding business, and I decided I needed help and guidance. Whilst I had grown the business successfully to that point, I certainly didn't want to lose it because of some fundamental mistakes that I hadn't yet learnt from.

COMMITMENT

As fate would have it, I was presented with an opportunity to join an inner circle of like-minded business owners and become part of a Mastermind Group. There were a couple of decisions that I had to make. Firstly, the monthly subscription was £1000 per month, and secondly, I had to commit time to attending seminars, one to one coaching sessions and accountability meetings. These were huge commitments both financially and timewise. Time, I could have been spending in my business.

As usual, I quickly took a decision to signing up to take advantage of this fantastic opportunity that had presented itself to me. I took on a new salesman that took care of the time issue and I also sold my brand-new Porsche (that did hurt a little) to help fund the salesman and the monthly subscription. I knew at the time that I was making a small sacrifice for bigger rewards further down the line. I also made a commitment to my fellow Mastermind colleagues that I would be there for them, to help and support them in both their business and personal lives.

DECISIONS

We are always presented with critical decisions that map out the journey of our life. These were three big decisions I had to make to give myself the best chance of success. When most people are presented with a decision to make, they shy away, slip back into their comfort zone and live the same year repeatedly, sticking to the status quo. I'm certainly not one of these people. My motto is "just do it", words that my fellow mastermind colleagues have heard many times in our mentoring sessions. Successful entrepreneurs make decisions quickly, and very rarely alter or change the decision once they make it. If you're serious about growing a successful business and earning and creating financial freedom, then I can guarantee you will have to make some difficult decisions along your journey.

Joining the Mastermind group over 4 years ago was one of the best decisions I have ever made. It has been incredibly important to me and with my hand on my heart, without the support from my friends and fellow entrepreneurs from within that group, my businesses wouldn't be where they are today. Sure, I have had to invest a lot of time and money to be a part of this, but I've gained invaluable advice and ideas I needed, whilst also helping other members to do the same.

Rather than just tell you how it worked for me I would like to show you the results it has given me in one particular company of mine.

2015 turnover – 188k

2016 turnover – 374k

2017 turnover – 904k

2018 turnover – 2.1 million

Don't get me wrong, it hasn't been easy, but I have implemented everything you will read in this book, which it has given me this kind of growth over the last 4 years. Whilst writing this, I'm about to launch my 4th business, so I'm doing something right!

With commitment comes sacrifice.

- What do you need to sacrifice to achieve your goals and visions?
- What decisions do you need to make?

ADVICE WITH VALUE

My advice is to always look at the bigger picture and not the here and now. Don't procrastinate and don't be afraid to give away something small to reap the bigger rewards further down the line.

Your life begins outside your comfort zone. Get comfortable being uncomfortable.

DEFINE AND GROW

Out of this chapter, here is your space to clarify your thinking, set your goals, chart the benefits, and hold yourself accountable in order to see your business and personal growth in action.

ACTION NEEDED	BENEFIT TO BUSINESS	IMPLEMENT BY (date)
1 _____	_____	__ / __ / __
_____	_____	
_____	_____	
2 _____	_____	__ / __ / __
_____	_____	
_____	_____	
3 _____	_____	__ / __ / __
_____	_____	
_____	_____	

NOTES

CHAPTER 3   WE DON'T KNOW, WHAT WE DON'T KNOW

LIFE-LONG LEARNING

Knowing what I know now, through experience and personal development, I'd certainly change the way I started my first business. Hindsight, what a wonderful thing!

This may sound odd to the average business owner who is consumed by his or her own business, but working on yourself is the next step as soon as you have a robust business plan in place.

Continuous learning, personal development or continuous professional development (CPD which is required in some professions), is the minimum requirement for success in any field. The majority of business owners believe, when they leave formal education, the learning stops. In my experience, it's where it really starts. Apart from basic maths and English, formal education may not have given some of us very much.

We're taught to memorise or copy what's in front of us (learning by rote). How much critical thinking or critical analysis did the teachers actually get us to do when we were in school? Not a lot, from memory.

Don't get me wrong, we learn some very good life skills and make friends along the way as we try to enjoy our school years, but my personal opinion is that the curriculum needs a shakeup. Whilst things may be changing, change is slow and is perhaps not keeping pace with what is needed, once out in the world of work.

Financial education is one area that would help everybody. We were never taught how to manage money at school, and not everyone is fortunate enough to come from a background that has sensible family members who can teach them how to manage a household budget, understand the APR on a credit card, or get to grips with savings plans and mortgage rates. Is there any wonder then when people end up in debt? We are not taught how to manage money or understand even basic finances. We have to make mistakes, so we can learn from them. Mistakes that could set us back years later with devastating consequences, in our adult lives. To overcome these limits, you have to make self-education and personal development a priority in your day to day activities.

The average business owner is destined to never hit their full potential because they are ignorant to the fact that they become the lid on their business. Because of their limited thinking, they are busy being busy, working *in* their business and not *on* their business. It's not their fault they've never been shown any other way. They started a business because they're experienced in that particular sector or skill. Their business is wrapped around them and doesn't function without them making decisions and eventually they become trapped in the business.

After years of building the business, it fails to gain any value because the business doesn't work without its owner. They effectively own a job and the chances of them selling the business and the financial return if they did could both be very low.

A smart business owner will think differently. They know that to be successful, in any field, you have to be prepared to do what others won't. This means working on oneself through personal growth and development, which in turn impacts both personal life and business growth. They understand their business is only as good as the thinking they bring to the table. Eventually, every entrepreneur's thinking peaks which in turn caps growth, both for them personally, and their business.

You don't have to be a seasoned entrepreneur. Treat your first business as an apprenticeship. You may know the product, service or trade in your chosen line of business, but running and growing a business is a whole new ball game and you don't know what you don't know. You must learn a whole new set of skills to help achieve your end game.

Remember, with each mistake you make, you gain the opportunity to build on that failure.

PERSONAL DEVELOPMENT

As an entrepreneur, for me personal growth is a non-negotiable daily habit. I have four different strategies which contribute to my personal development.

STRATEGY 1 - READING

Each year I set myself a personal goal to read 24 books. I achieve this by reading for 1 hour a day. I wake up early, make a cup of coffee, and dedicate the first hour of my day to personal growth. I read a range of business, personal growth and mindset books. Some of the world's most successful entrepreneurs, such as Bill Gates, make reading part of their daily routine. On average he reads four books a month, so I need to up my game! What a fine example Bill Gates is. He's one of the richest men in the world, yet still looks to improve on the wealth of knowledge he already has.

Some of the great books I have read, have helped and inspired me to implement the strategies offered in these pages. I've also read a couple of books that have bored the living hell out of me and I couldn't wait to finish, but I've always persevered, stayed focused and seen the book through to the end. This is because there's always a chance of a golden nugget of information that just might impact my thinking or business.

My top 5 books that I'd recommend anyone read are:

1. Think and Grow Rich, by Napoleon Hill
2. Built to Sell, by John Warrillow
3. The e-Myth, by Michael E Gerber
4. The One Thing, by Gary W Keller
5. The 7 Habits of Highly Effective People, by Stephen Covey

GOLDEN NUGGET

Reading may not be for everyone, but with technology at our disposal, there are many different ways to "read" a book. For instance, listening to audiobooks and podcasts is something I do when I'm on the treadmill in the gym or travelling long journeys in the car. Start with a small goal of one book or audio book a month. The aim is to make reading a daily habit. It takes 30 days for an activity to become a habit. During these 30 days your commitment will be tested to its limits, so stick with it.

STRATEGY 2 - MASTERMIND GROUP

Being an entrepreneur and owning your own business can be a very lonely place at times. Where, or who, do you turn to for help, guidance or advice? Most may turn to their friends or family, or even Joe Blogs down the pub. Whoever you turn to you can pretty much guarantee they will not be qualified to answer the questions you pose to them, and all they can offer is an opinion on what they think is right or what they think you want to hear.

This is where seeking a more structured form of help can be invaluable to helping you on your personal development journey. For me, joining the 729 Renegade Mastermind Group was the best decision I've ever made. My business has grown 200% and my personal life has improved dramatically.

They are the Board I couldn't afford. I had nine other entrepreneurs to help with my challenges and also guidance for me and my businesses.

At our first 3 day summit, we all started off as complete strangers, by the end of our time together, we left as friends. These people are entrepreneurs, some in the infancy of their journeys, and some who are experienced and successful. What impressed me most about the group was the breadth of experience. I realised that everyone had something individual and brilliant to bring to the table. We're all go-getters and are there to help each other stretch our thinking and grow our businesses. It's great to be a part of everyone's journey, seeing them grow and develop knowing that you've contributed to their success. There's no better feeling than giving back and helping people achieve their goal and visions.

All very highly successful entrepreneurs are in Mastermind Groups; Buffet, Gates and Branson to name a few. Napoleon Hill's book 'Think and Grow Rich' has helped make more millionaires than any other book in history. He explains a mastermind process best by saying:

"The mastermind may be defined as coordination of knowledge and effort, in a spirit of harmony between two or more people, for the attainment of a definite purpose".

Imagine the power of ten minds working in perfect harmony, working on your goals and visions. During this process, you hit a different level of awareness. You're consciously thinking and educating each other, ten different viewpoints in relation to one question; all from experienced entrepreneurs. That's the true power of participating in a Mastermind Group.

Mastermind Groups have been around for many years and only seem to be for highly successful people. It feels like it's been a big secret between the highly successful. Well, if you're reading this then it's no longer a secret.

Opportunities to join groups do not come around often. This maybe the first time you've ever read or heard about one. I would advise any business owner who wants to enjoy a fulfilled life and achieve financial freedom to join one and watch you and your business grow.

STRATEGY 3 – A COACH OR MENTOR

Whether you're a new start up or looking to grow your business, then having a coach or a mentor should be a part of your apprenticeship as a business owner. A coach/mentor will help get the best out of you. They ask you questions you don't know how to ask yourself and help you dig deep for answers. A coach is usually someone that will work with you for a short period of time in a more formal and structured manner, whilst a mentor is more suited to a longer term informal process and a relationship built on trust and respect.

Whichever you decide to choose, it's important to bear in mind that sometimes we can't always see the bigger picture when we're in the frame, especially when we're juggling a million and one things to keep everyone and everything going.

Why do we need a coach or mentor? Look at sport, every successful team or individual will have a coach. When you were learning your trade, you were coached or mentored. A coach or mentor will guide and advice to help us become the best we can be. They've probably already experienced things you haven't even thought about.

Leverage that experience to help you and your business avoid pitfalls before they happen. If you speak to any successful entrepreneur, I'll guarantee they have a coach/mentor, maybe not right from the start but somewhere along the way they realised that they needed help.

A word of advice, there are a lot of self-proclaimed business coaches and I would recommend you do your research on any you resonate with, before you deem them fit to help you. Do they have their own business? Have they grown a business from start-up stage? Have they had experience employing people? Have they failed in business? These are all pluses in my opinion because they've experienced failure, which in turn brings key experience. In the UK we see failure as a bad thing. When someone fails in business, it's not the end of the world. We need to flip our thinking because from failure comes invaluable experience. Experience that you certainly cannot buy, but you can share with others, to help them avoid making the same mistake.

Around 4 years ago, I hit a point in my business where I knew I needed help to scale. I found two business coaches, did my due diligence on both and decided to invest in one of them. From a personal and business point of view it was one of the most important and best decisions I've made to date. Having a coach gives me 1-1 coaching with the day to day challenges I face. My coach has a wealth of experience which I leverage to my benefit and that is priceless.

STRATEGY 4 - MODELLING SUCCESSFUL PEOPLE

We have many different role models in our life. Sports stars, movie stars and singers to name but a few. When we see, hear and listen to these people, we can't help but feel motivated and inspired. Modelling successful people in business is a great way to get an insight on how things could be done. They don't even have to be in the same industry as your chosen profession.

I don't use social media a lot, but every morning when I've finished my hour of reading, I sit down in my sun room at home, with my phone in one hand, coffee in the other and I have a flick through Instagram.

Firstly, I am very selective with regards to who I follow on Instagram. In fact, the only people I follow are the ones that inspire and motivate me. I follow a whole range of different people from successful entrepreneurs to top sports stars and even daily motivational quotes.

Every morning I fill my subconscious mind with this energy that helps set me up for the day. Reading a quote or just looking at a photograph really does help get me motivated. It's a true saying, 'we always want that we can't have'.

My philosophy is, if I want it, I get up and chase it until I get it.

When I first started out in business, my role model was my former and last ever boss, David. He was a successful entrepreneur with several different businesses and a portfolio of properties. I had the pleasure of working with him for 7 years, from being an apprentice to throughout the years when I learned my skills, before stepping up to a supervisory role and then on to management. I pretty much served my time in every department to make it to the top.

Once at the top and working alongside David, he gave me some very good advice. He said, "Learn what you can from me, as quickly as you can. I won't be around forever and anything I have at my disposal; I'll happily share with you".

David knew my ambition was to develop my own company, but here we had a win/win for both of us. I delivered some of the biggest projects in the company's history, and made him a few quid along the way, as well as learning how to run a business in my chosen trade. I was fortunate enough to draw 7 years of wisdom and experience from this guy before I went on my way.

Being the man he was, David also helped me when I first started up. He let me keep my van, tools, laptop and phone, as well as giving me an envelope with some money in it, to help me get started. For this I'll always be very grateful. I still speak to him today and on many occasions pick up the phone for some free advice.

Ask yourself the questions:

- How much do you value yourself to dedicate an hour a day to learn, improve and grow?
- How much do you value your business success to consider hiring a coach or mentor?

DEFINE AND GROW

Out of this chapter, here is your space to clarify your thinking, set your goals, chart the benefits, and hold yourself accountable in order to see your business and personal growth in action.

ACTION NEEDED	BENEFIT TO BUSINESS	IMPLEMENT BY (date)
1 _____	_____	__ / __ / __
_____	_____	
_____	_____	
2 _____	_____	__ / __ / __
_____	_____	
_____	_____	
3 _____	_____	__ / __ / __
_____	_____	
_____	_____	

NOTES

CHAPTER 4   VISIONS AND GOALS

WHAT'S YOUR VISION?

A big part of the personal development process is visioning. As you learn more and grow yourself you'll realise how important it is to have a vision for both your personal and business life. All successful people have one and it's the next part of the building block in growing a successful company.

According to the dictionary; vison means:

'The ability to think about or plan the future with imagination or wisdom'

There are 2 forms of vision that I want you to concentrate on. One is your *personal vision* and the other is your *company vision*. This is what we mean when we say, 'start with the end game in mind'. This will require some deep, hard thinking. We tend to look for easy options or for somebody to tell us what to do. Thinking for yourself means that you're in control of your own destiny.

Your vision will be the road map you will use to get to your end destination, your own personal satnav which is why we start with our end game in mind. If you're particularly keen to work on this further and delve deeper, then I highly recommend the book 'Think and Grow Rich' by Napoleon Hill.

For now though, to start a simple visioning process, all you need is somewhere quiet; a pen, a pad and a desire to see into your future. Try it, and then make it a daily routine, taking a minimum of 30 minutes out of your busy schedule to vision.

Visioning is daydreaming while documenting your thoughts. No one can tell you your thoughts. Everything you want, or need is inside of you. You must dig deep and draw it out by stretching your thinking. You'll know if you have had a good visioning session because you will be exhausted from thinking.

Don't expect that your vision will be done in one session, and don't heap too much pressure on yourself to get it right first time. I remember when I wrote my visions, in total to perfect, it took me around 4 weeks and that was visioning for 30 minutes a day. Again, for me I found that visioning on awakening first thing in a morning while everyone else was still asleep worked best for me. Find what works best for you.

PERSONAL VISION:

Your personal vision should consist of personal aspirations that can be measured by goal setting. By using goals, you can monitor the journey by hitting milestones to make sure you're on track. Include family and friends as well, after all I'm pretty sure you're not looking for a better life just for yourself. Share your vision with whom it will affect. This will help people close to you, understand why you may be working long hours or sacrificing something that doesn't align with what you want to achieve.

COMPANY VISION:

Your company vision should consist of the aspiration of what you want your company to achieve and be measured by goal setting. Once you have a company vision, sharing it with your staff is equally important. They are on the journey with you and you need to tell them where they are heading. This is a common mistake some business owners make. You may not find the average business owner with a company vision, as they are just riding their luck; hoping things will work out.

Our thinking is only as good as the questions we are prepared to ask ourselves. So here are a few questions to get the juices flowing:

1. What's your purpose in life?
2. How do you want to be remembered?
3. How can you affect the lives of others for the good?

4. How much money do I require to reach financial freedom?

5. What are your personal and business goals?

6. What is your legacy?

Asking and answering questions like this will help you think about what you really want from life, and once you have the answers, you then have a plan and a road map for your life. A vision without execution is pointless. You need to have a burning desire to want to achieve what you have written. Whatever your vision looks like, make sure it excites you to get up in a morning and want to go to work on it.

GOALS

Goal setting is a way of measuring and keeping track of your vision. All your goals should be aligned with your vision. Goals should be a mixture of both short and long-term goals. Even throw in some 'BeHAGs' - big hairy audacious goals.

I personally have a strategy session once a year in December. I book a conference/meeting room at a local hotel. I make sure the room is nice and quiet without any distractions. I turn off my phone and don't let anything or anyone distract me for the full day. I request a flip chart, paper and plenty of ink and then I start to visualise the year ahead. This is something I certainly didn't know when I started my first business. Self-education has taught me that it's now one of the most important days of the year for me, and I know it can be for you too.

Some of the questions you can ask yourself in your strategy sessions might be:

1. What do you want your company to achieve in year one?

2. What turnover do you want?

3. What staff/resources do you need and when do you need them by?

4. How many customers do you need in year one?

Think hard, stay focused and I'll guarantee you that when you leave that room after 8 hours, you'll have clarity on the goals and visions for your business that will serve you for the next 12 months. If you can answer questions like this, then you can use the information to set your goals. A strategy session should be an annual event where you can think about setting the next years' goals.

Once you have a plan, it's important to share it with anyone else involved in the business. Call a meeting and explain how and what your visions and goals are for the next 12 months. Make everyone feel a part of it. Where do they fit in? Make sure everyone is on board, so the whole company pulls in the same direction. Finally, put up a visual board or chart in the office and add each goal for everyone to see. Once that goal is achieved, mark them off and throughout the year the whole company can see the progression they make.

So far we have covered some of the basic foundations required to build a successful business. Let's now look at other areas we need to cover before we're ready to open the doors.

DEFINE AND GROW

Out of this chapter, here is your space to clarify your thinking, set your goals, chart the benefits, and hold yourself accountable in order to see your business and personal growth in action.

ACTION NEEDED	BENEFIT TO BUSINESS	IMPLEMENT BY (date)
1 _____	_____	__ / __ / __
_____	_____	
_____	_____	
2 _____	_____	__ / __ / __
_____	_____	
_____	_____	
3 _____	_____	__ / __ / __
_____	_____	
_____	_____	

NOTES

You may read this and think, this all sounds good, but I just don't have the time. This is where a well-structured and organised day comes into play.

We all have the same 24 hours in a day; the difference is how we choose to spend these 24 hours. Delegation is one of the key factors to creating time. One quick win that you can implement very easily and quickly is a "TO DO" list. This is a list of daily activities that are currently on your schedule that you're able to pass on to somebody else to execute.

Don't be afraid of delegating tasks to others; this is a win/win situation. Once you've taken the time to create the list and shown somebody else how to execute it, you have cleared time in your schedule for some personal growth and development time.

Time is the most important thing we have and how you spend this time, will show in the results you see in your personal life and business. Be consciously aware of how you spend your time and make sure it aligns with your goals and vision.

Educating yourself requires some form of financial investment from you. This must be viewed as an investment and not as a cost. I personally spend over 20k a year on self-education and personal development. My return on investment shows up in my results.

All my businesses have seen a minimum of 100% increase in turn over year on year. Our businesses are only as good as the quality of thinking we bring to them. Participating in self-education and personal growth will develop your thinking and improve your results.

A typical start up business in its infancy starts like this.

Let's say you are a plumber for instance, you served an apprenticeship and you were trained in how to install pipe work, boilers etc. You're the best plumber in the UK who's working for somebody else.

Then you decide to set up your own business, which is great and well done for preparing to step out of your comfort zone and into the unknown. However, you have never had a business before, so how do you know how to run the business? The simple answer is, you don't.

You've never been shown this side of your trade. So, you end up becoming a technician within your business. Yes, you're getting paid more money, but more money means more stress and more problems to deal with. Your business only earns money when you're installing or fixing problems.

You don't run the business; the business runs you. This isn't what you signed up for. You don't want to be a technician; you want to be the entrepreneur with the company vision, but you don't have time. There it is again, that short little word that's so important to us; time.

One of my fellow mastermind colleagues has a great analogy of what we must do as business owners and it will stay with me forever.

'Your business is like a ship. The captain needs to be on the bridge to steer the ship and co-ordinate its movements. Now and again the captain may need to go below deck to help shovel some coal to keep the engines fuelled. However, the captain must make it a priority to return to the bridge to take back control of the ship to get to the destination they're travelling to.'

Are you an entrepreneur or are you a technician?

Are you the Captain or the engineer?

Growing a business is a journey. There's no such thing as overnight success. It's up to you to go and chase your dreams. If you wake up in a morning and you don't have a dream to chase, go back to the drawing board until you find something worth jumping out of bed for.

You need to be able to enjoy your journey. Every day is a stepping stone to where we want to be. This is your vision. Without a vision for your personal life and business life you will just exist. Write down a plan for both. Articulate it in your mind and get emotionally involved.

Once you have this, you'll attract all resources you need to achieving success. Share the vision with your employees, get them involved and get them believing in your vision. What does it look like for them, how will they benefit?

DEFINE AND GROW

Out of this chapter, here is your space to clarify your thinking, set your goals, chart the benefits, and hold yourself accountable in order to see your business and personal growth in action.

ACTION NEEDED	BENEFIT TO BUSINESS	IMPLEMENT BY (date)
1 _____	_____	___ / ___ / ___
_____	_____	
_____	_____	
2 _____	_____	___ / ___ / ___
_____	_____	
_____	_____	
3 _____	_____	___ / ___ / ___
_____	_____	
_____	_____	

NOTES

CHAPTER 6 — YOUR GREATEST ASSETS ARE YOUR EMPLOYEES

If you are anything other than a sole trader then your employees are the backbone of your business. How much time and effort do you invest in them? Grow your employees and you will grow your business.

I wrote earlier about the importance of your own personal development, but you also need to commit to training and developing your employees.

I give all my staff a book to read every month. They return the book on payday. No book return, no pay. I hold them accountable, so we both know it will get done. In exchange, they benefit by reading 12 books a year and are better placed to grow in our business and earn more money.

This is set out at interview stage. I want to know whether they'll buy in from the start and be committed to personal growth. If both owner and staff are continuously learning and educating themselves on a daily basis, your results in life will only be heading in the right direction.

It's all well and good to read articles and books like this but we must implement what we are learning. Personal development is a choice. A choice you as an individual have to make. Your own self-awareness of what you really want to achieve in life.

What changes must you make in your daily activities to help you achieve your dreams?

Remember, self-development is a process and not an event. It's a continuous process of carrying out personal growth activity and implementing what we learn.

Develop your employees to develop your business. Just as the owner of the business, where you can put a lid on your business by not developing yourself on a consistent basis, it's the same for your employees. They are only as good as the skills and thinking they currently have. If you're not investing in your employees, then how can they develop and in turn, how can the business develop.

A favourite and inspiring quote of mine is "the more you learn the more you earn."

ADVICE WITH VALUE

We all learn in different ways and at different speeds. Find what works best to enable you to become the best version of yourself.

DEFINE AND GROW

Out of this chapter, here is your space to clarify your thinking, set your goals, chart the benefits, and hold yourself accountable in order to see your business and personal growth in action.

ACTION NEEDED	BENEFIT TO BUSINESS	IMPLEMENT BY (date)
1 _____	_____	__ / __ / __
_____	_____	
_____	_____	
2 _____	_____	__ / __ / __
_____	_____	
_____	_____	
3 _____	_____	__ / __ / __
_____	_____	
_____	_____	

NOTES

On the cover of Renegade magazine – masterminds

Proud father Dean with his beautiful twin girls Ellie and Grace in his office.

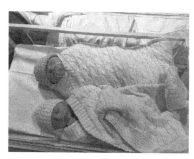

The happy arrival of two daughters in 2019

Mia and Kia enjoying the home view

Fresh air stroll with the twin girls and four-legged family in the neighbourhood

Treasured family and friends

*The premises of Concept
Pools, with Tanqua Pools in
the next door unit*

Team spirit – the Concept group

2012 London Olympics swimming pool, and plant room

CHAPTER 7   ROLES AND RESPONSIBILITIES IN YOUR BUSINESS

Behind every successful business is a well thought out structure: a structure of your people and how your business is structured internally. A good structure is based on the foundations you put in place from day one of the business. Who's responsible for each department and what their role is within the business. In this chapter I'll go into more detail along with how important employees are to the success of any business.

At this point you may be the only person in your business, but this doesn't stop you creating an employee organisation structure as shown below.

Start with a blank piece of paper and right at the top centre of the page, draw a square box, and in that box, write Director and your name inside it. You are top of the organisation structure because you are the owner and (hopefully) major shareholder. As you've already thought about and written your company vision, you'll know how many different positions you'll need to fill with employees for both present and the future. For now, you may find that you have your name in every position within your company, but don't worry, the good thing is that you'll identify the positions that need to be filled with other people (employees).

Director/Your Name		
Head of Finance	**Head of Sales**	**Head of Production**
Your Name	Your Name	Your Name
Book Keeper 1: Your Name	Salesman 1: Your Name	Production worker 1: Your Name
	Salesman 2: Your Name	Production worker 2: Your Name
		Production worker 3: Your Name
		Production worker 4: Your Name

As new employees come in to fill the positions, keep the structure updated and visible for everyone to see. For example, below I have used an organisation structure from one of my businesses, Concept Pools. It identifies management positions with technicians below them in varied positions.

Director/Dean Thistleton			
Head of Finance	Head of Service	Head of Contracts	Head of Sales/Marketing
Adam Thorpe	Andy Thistleton	Dave Nightingale	Adam Moffatt
Book Keeper 1	Service Engineer 1	Installation Engineer 1	Salesman 1
	Service Engineer 2	Installation Engineer 2	
	Service Engineer 3	Installation Engineer 3	
	Service Engineer 4	Installation Engineer 4	

At the top we have me, Director/major shareholder. Underneath me we have management positions, which we prefer to refer to as Heads of Departments. These are leadership positions which include coaching and mentoring employees they are responsible for within the company.

Next are the individual employees for each department, the technicians of the business. So, in total we have 4 management positions and 9 technician positions. This structure is based on a service business with a turnover of 2.5 million pounds to give you an idea of staff required versus turnover. Every business will be different, but this will give you an idea of what you might need as you scale.

For each position, roles and responsibilities are carefully thought about and written. These responsibilities can vary from who is responsible for acquiring a new service contract, to simple things like, who keeps the coffee and milk topped up in the kitchen.

If responsibilities are clarified and written down on a document by you at the start and then given to each employee to read, understand and sign, then this should get your people singing from the same hymn sheet and help the businesses run more smoothly and efficiently with a high level of control.

MANAGING THE NUMBERS

So, who would be your first employee within your structure? I think you'll be very surprised with what I'm about to share with you. The first person through the door as your first employee should be Head of Finance. Somebody who can take care of the money, invoices, suppliers, banks, setting up of supplier accounts, chasing outstanding invoices, just to name a few of the tasks involved within this role.

If you're like me, I hate numbers and wasn't very good at maths. I think I walked out of school with an E in Maths, so numbers are not my strongest point. This is why I only employ people who are better than me.

The tasks and work involved in the accounts department is often overlooked and is not on the top of everyone's list when you're starting out, but from my experience they should be the first employee, even if it's only part time.

Often start-ups will say to themselves, well I can do the invoicing and supplier bills at night time or on weekends. But if this isn't your strength, then why would you want to do it. You should be concentrating on the activities that earn you more money, activities that only you can do.

If employing someone to do the accounts puts you off or you can't afford them, then a good option would be to find somebody part time to start with. Maybe someone who has retired and is looking for some extra income on top of their pension, but most importantly has the skill and experience you don't have.

ADVICE WITH VALUE

Employees are the heartbeat of any thriving business. Finding the right people for the right positions is probably one of the hardest tasks a business has to undertake.

DEFINE AND GROW

Out of this chapter, here is your space to clarify your thinking, set your goals, chart the benefits, and hold yourself accountable in order to see your business and personal growth in action.

ACTION NEEDED	BENEFIT TO BUSINESS	IMPLEMENT BY (date)
1 _____	_____	__ / __ / __
_____	_____	
_____	_____	
2 _____	_____	__ / __ / __
_____	_____	
_____	_____	
3 _____	_____	__ / __ / __
_____	_____	
_____	_____	

NOTES

FINDING TALENTED PEOPLE

Over the years I've learned to be constantly on the lookout for new talent. One of my core values when it comes to recruiting is to only employ people who are better than me. I only look for 'A' players. It's not about putting bums on seats, you're not always going to get your recruitment right, but sometimes you just know if the person is a good fit or not. Knowing and understanding your company culture and values will give you a better success rate.

For me, you have to consciously be on the lookout for new talent, even when you don't have any positions to fill. You can be anywhere, a restaurant, clothes shop, out at family gatherings, at meetings with suppliers for instance.

One of my best salesmen was originally working as a rep for one of our key suppliers. He came in for a meeting to upsell a new product. During the meeting I thought to myself, I like this guy, his attitude and the way he came across resonated with me. Bearing in mind, at the time he was working for a 2 billion turnover company, and here I was thinking about wanting to employ him. Later that week I planted the seed with him via a telephone call. I then followed this up with an informal meeting where we discussed our goals and vision for the company and most importantly, where I could see him fitting in to help us grow and develop the business.

At the time I wasn't really looking for a salesman, so I created the position within the company because I knew this guy could help us scale and scale fast. So, within one month of planting a seed, we had officially started our first salesman. Salesmen are not really the industry norm, so we were going into unchartered waters, which felt brilliant. Twelve months later and he had hit all the targets and goals we set out for him and is currently in the process of developing a sales team underneath him.

To attract the best people you need to be proactive. Building a team of 'A' players can be challenging, but also very rewarding and once you have the right people in the right places, that you can delegate authority to, you have time to work on the business rather than in it.

Our best recruits have come via LinkedIn and Indeed and on these platforms you can choose to advertise either with recruitment posts or sponsored ads. You can target specific people and with the ability to control how much you spend by setting a daily/weekly budget, you can stop a campaign at any time.

We get approached by agencies pretty much every day but personally, I'm not a fan of using them. The fees they charge can be extortionate to say the least, and who's to say they won't come back for your employee in the future when another company is looking to fill a similar position.

KEEPING YOUR TALENTED WORKFORCE

Let's face it; people come to work to earn money. As business owners and employers it is important to provide an environment where employees can enjoy their work whilst being compensated for their efforts. This remuneration can come in various different ways, such as holiday entitlement, pay raises and bonuses to name a few.

Every December I give all our employees a bonus and also a pay rise. Even I get one. This instantly brings a feel-good factor to each individual, which transcends into the company re-start in January. All the staff come back to work and hit the ground running and there's a general feel-good factor around the company. Everyone is pulling together and giving their all, ready for the year ahead. For me this is a worthwhile investment every December.

STAFF EQUITY

As you scale and start to add key staff into your business to relieve you of some of the important day to day activities, then a way of securing and keeping hold of key staff is what we call staff equity.

This is a profit share of the year end accounts and I have this in all my businesses. In my first business I gave away 40% of my profits to key two members of staff. They both received 20% each. They've both helped me scale the business in a way that I couldn't have done on my own. Even though they are entitled to 20% each of the profits, I still own 100% of the business as I am the only share holder.

If you were to choose this route with any future staff members, it's absolutely paramount that you do the following.

Within the employee contract make sure that the staff member is only entitled to the profit share based on performance at your discretion. I failed to do this the first time I allowed profit share and it backfired. If the person entitled to have the profit share isn't putting in the extra commitment and performing as you would expect for their share, then the power is still in your hands to decide if they deserve a share of the hard-earned profits.

EMPLOYEE SUPPORT

Employing people can be a roller coaster ride. In May 2017 one of my engineers was out at the weekend, riding his motor cross bike on a track. He came off the bike and broke his neck as well as picking up a few other injuries. Thankfully none of it was life-threatening and he's since gone to make a full recovery.

When something like this happens, as an employer, you have several different reactions. The first thought is, I hope he's ok. Then you realise you're going to be a man down and he'll need replacing, which will cost money. But you also need to look after the guy who's laid up in bed incapacitated. What I did in this instance was find out how much his bills were and made sure we covered them until he returned to work 3 months later.

I'm guessing there aren't many companies that would be so supporting under the circumstances. On his return to work I think he felt somehow indebted to us for sticking by him. He's back at work and has gone the extra mile on many occasions, not only working very hard but earning himself a promotion within the company with an 8k pay rise.

All employees are an investment. They lighten my work load and help scale the business year on year. I am truly thankful for the people I have and I make everyone a promise when they start work for me. A promise I'll help them create a better life for themselves and their families. I tell them that as the company grows, so will the benefits of being part of it. They're not just a number on the payroll. They are part of a family.

DEFINE AND GROW

Out of this chapter, here is your space to clarify your thinking, set your goals, chart the benefits, and hold yourself accountable in order to see your business and personal growth in action.

ACTION NEEDED	BENEFIT TO BUSINESS	IMPLEMENT BY (date)
1 _____	_____	__ / __ / __
_____	_____	
_____	_____	
2 _____	_____	__ / __ / __
_____	_____	
_____	_____	
3 _____	_____	__ / __ / __
_____	_____	
_____	_____	

NOTES

CHAPTER 9   PROCEDURE, PROCESS AND SYSTEMS

SYSTEMS

Every business needs good reliable, ways of doing things. Having procedures, processes and systems in place will help your business run smoothly and efficiently, which in turn leads to better profitability. Sounds good doesn't it? Often when procedure, process and systems are mentioned to start-up businesses, you can see their eyes glaze over in fear. Like a lot of things in life, some people over-think and over-complicate things they have never experienced before. Rome wasn't built in a day, and neither is a business. A business can take 10 years to be an 'overnight' success.

When considering how and where to begin, start with something easy that can be quickly put in place and that is going to be used often. This allows you to quickly see the benefit of having taken the time to create it in the first place. Oh, and whatever systems you deploy – remember to include adequate training for staff to allow them to adapt and become efficient in the use of new working practices.

Below we are going to look at **procedures and processes** and **online software systems**

PROCEDURES AND PROCESSES

All procedures and processes should be easy to follow instructions of how to execute a task within a business. These can either be written instructions or, if preferred, video content.

The instructions should be a step by step guide of how to do a particular task. They should be written instructions that are clear and easy to follow, so much so that a stranger could execute a particular task within your business without asking for help.

As a start-up business, you may not yet have any procedures or processes in place, but the trick is to start writing down or recording the tasks you are carrying out, so when you have employees in the near future, these tasks can be delegated to them. The aim is to create an operation manual for the business where all procedures and processes can be found.

This becomes very handy if the usual person that, let's say, books the courier is off sick. With a comprehensive operation manual, any other member of staff can follow the procedure as laid out and arrange the courier booking.

As you scale the business and the staff members increase, so do the activities within the business. Don't be afraid to let employees write/document the activity to be included in the manual. Once each new procedure and process is written, test this by letting someone else follow the instructions created, to prove it works.

Here's an example of how to book a courier, for one of my companies. This shows you how basic simple instructions written down can create an easy to follow process. It details how to book in and arrange a collection by our courier service for a product that has to be delivered to a customer.

Working Procedure: Book a Delivery with Courier

Log in to TNT account: www.tnt.com

Enter user ID: xxxx@concept-pools.co.uk

Enter Password: xxxxxxxxxx

1. Create Shipment.
2. To make things easy, have the postcode of delivery destination. Input this into postcode and TNT will automatically find address. Select the correct address.
3. Input details and phone number of the receiver.

4. Enter description of goods.

5. Add shipment value.

6. Select package type you are sending.

7. Input quantity, weight, length, width and height.

8. Press 'Continue'.

9. Selections. Select pick up time and latest pick up time. If you don't want the driver there in between certain hours select "Not between" hours.

10. Choose price.

11. Select email address you want the documents to be sent to.

12. Press 'Continue'.

13. Print off documents. On standard order there should be 3 documents. 1 bar code to stick on the box/item being delivered. The 2 other documents are for the TNT driver to sign on collection. 1 copy for Concept Pools and 1 for the TNT driver.

14. All done.

As you can see this document is very simple and self-explanatory but very effective. So easy, that even I've used it when I needed an urgent delivery to be sent out on a Friday evening when everyone had gone home for the weekend. It was the first time I'd ever booked in a delivery, and I'm glad to say it all worked out. The delivery was picked up and delivered to the customer.

ONLINE SOFTWARE SYSTEMS:

There are some very good cost-effective software programmes on the market to help us manage and control our business at a click of a button.

Some examples of software packages are:

- Xero - an accounting software package
- Pipedrive - a sales software package
- Ontraport - a CRM software package for marketing
- Team Up Calendar - a calendar to help manage staff movements.

All of these systems can be paid for by monthly subscription, which helps with cash flow. In this day and age, we have to use technology to our advantage. For example, the Xero accounting software package, when integrated into our business, was a revelation and helped me personally to see in real time, our key financial information. Some of the key benefits of the Xero system are:

- Invoicing: Keep your cash flow healthy by sending online invoices with online payment options
- Dashboard: See how cash is tracking with a quick glance at your customisable Xero dashboard
- Pay bills: Pay bills on time, reduce office admin and improve your cash flow
- VAT online: Make life easy for your small business with online VAT processing in Xero
- Business performance dashboard: Get the full up-to-date picture of how your business is performing

This accounting software has been designed for small businesses and will benefit you and your business in many different ways. It's imperative to understand the numbers in your business and having systems like this will help you understand your financial position and help making important decision a lot easier and simpler.

There will be many more systems that you'll need to add in to the business as you scale but if you start by getting the important fundamental ones in place at the start, then it'll give you a good solid foundation for the future and an understanding of how important systems are to a successful business.

DEFINE AND GROW

Out of this chapter, here is your space to clarify your thinking, set your goals, chart the benefits, and hold yourself accountable in order to see your business and personal growth in action.

ACTION NEEDED	BENEFIT TO BUSINESS	IMPLEMENT BY (date)
1 _____	_____	__ / __ / __
_____	_____	
_____	_____	
2 _____	_____	__ / __ / __
_____	_____	
_____	_____	
3 _____	_____	__ / __ / __
_____	_____	
_____	_____	

NOTES

CHAPTER 10   MARKETING

Marketing has become much easier than in the past – and it has to be a business priority. A lot of marketing campaigns can be automated once initially set up. Yes, this will cost money and time, but don't look at it as a cost, see it more as an investment.

There are 2 types of online marketing: - Interruption marketing and attraction marketing.

Interruption, for example, is a Facebook ad targeted to you while you are browsing the newsfeeds. An example of attraction marketing would be Google 'pay per click' where the customer is actively looking to buy/research your product or service.

If you're not marketing your business, then you're losing out on a huge number of potential customers.

MARKETING FOR NEW CUSTOMERS

When a typical business owner thinks of marketing, his limiting belief system says to him, "oh no, this means I have to spend money", which is true, but we have to change our belief and mindset. A mindset change to one of investment. We're in the business of buying customers.

Not only do we have to spend money, but also give away information for free to help educate and build the trust to develop a relationship with a potential customer. We can target our potential customers by both online and offline marketing. Yes, we live in a world where the internet is a very powerful and easy way to target your audience, but there's also an audience waiting offline.

While everyone else is focused on online marketing there are a large proportion of customers waiting to have something delivered through the door. This is where direct mail comes in. People still love getting things in the post that they can touch and feel. But, as with any marketing, we need to test and measure to see what the results are telling us.

How many marketing strategies do you currently have in place? Any business should have at least 8 different forms of marketing.

Here are just a few:

Pay per click

Direct response marketing

Social media marketing

Telephone marketing

Direct mail marketing through the post

TV & Radio advertising

The aim is to get started. Test everything and see what gives you the best returns. However, marketing is changing at a fast speed so be open minded for new and different ways to market to your potential customers. Different strategies work for different businesses in different industries. Find what works for you and as with everything in business, it's a process.

For me, Google pay per click is by far the most effective for the wet leisure industry. However, we should always test and measure to see what works and what doesn't. Along the way to finding out what works, we have spent a lot of time and money, but this hasn't been in vain as we now know our best ways to reach our customers.

DEFINE AND GROW

Out of this chapter, here is your space to clarify your thinking, set your goals, chart the benefits, and hold yourself accountable in order to see your business and personal growth in action.

ACTION NEEDED	BENEFIT TO BUSINESS	IMPLEMENT BY (date)
1 _____	_____	__ / __ / __
_____	_____	
_____	_____	
2 _____	_____	__ / __ / __
_____	_____	
_____	_____	
3 _____	_____	__ / __ / __
_____	_____	
_____	_____	

NOTES

CHAPTER 11   TURNING AN IDEA INTO A PRODUCT

During my time writing this book, I had a breakthrough on a new product which in turn is going to be a new business venture.

Last year I was sitting on a sun lounger in Dubai (the best ideas come to you when you're relaxed, especially in the sunshine). I lay there thinking about a gap in the market between a hot tub and a domestic swimming pool and there is undoubtedly a large financial cost between the two. My thinking turned to a more affordable pool and the outcome of my thoughts was to turn a shipping container into a swimming pool. How hard could that be? It does seem easy when you're sat in 35-degree heat with a beer in your hand.

The more I thought about it, the more the engineering side of my brain kicked in and a plan of how we would build them started to formulate. This idea was achievable and being a shipping container, we could ship it around the world. Whoop pass me another beer!

On my return from holiday I knew I had a good idea - but was it a business? A mini business plan was quickly put together and the numbers were crunched. Sell 12 of these in the first year and we have the foundation for a good profitable business to build on. Within a month of my return, the business plan stacked up and a decision was made to build the prototype and just do it.

There were going to be two size options for the container pools, 20ft long and 40ft long as these were two standard sizes of shipping containers. We like a challenge so we ordered a brand new 40ft shipping container to be delivered to the factory. Because this was our first build, we didn't have any staff to carry out any of the works.

I quickly assembled a team that we needed to get the job done. This team was me, my contracts manager from another business and a welder/fabricator who I knew from school days. We all had other commitments so could only work on the container at night time and weekends. The main thing was that we were all on-board and prepared to do whatever it took to produce our first container pool.

We produced a 3D AutoCAD image of how we wanted the container pool to look as a finished article. All the internal parts were sketched up on how we thought it would go together along with a process of what needed to be done at each stage of the build. We were in a perfect 'fake it until you make it' situation. We had to go for it and fight the challenges head on.

I could have pondered over this idea for a long time without taking any action to execute it, but if I didn't do it, you can guarantee somebody else would. So, we began to push on with the works. There were a few major challenges and some nights we would work for 4 or 5 hours and by the end of it we were altering or taking out what we had built. One step forward, two steps back was mentioned a few times. The main thing was we were learning how to do it and how not to do it.

After 10 weeks of building, it was time to test the pool and fill with water.

At first test we had around 400mm of water in the bottom and had to empty to fix a leak. After fixing the leak we did a second test, this time we filled the pool to the top and noticed the top edge of the pool had deflected with the weight of the water – a problem we didn't foresee. We believed the steel was sized correctly but we had deflection. Although it wasn't a lot, I'm a perfectionist and we had to do something about it. So, we had no choice but to empty the pool and add more steel around the top edge and perimeter to stiffen up the top which would stop any deflection, this also meant adding more decking around the perimeter as well as a re-spraying the outside of the container.

With these works complete, we once again filled the pool with water, and with our fingers crossed there would be no leaks or deflection in the steel work.

After 4 days of filling and constant checking, the pool was finally full. Next, we fired up the filtration system to check all pipes, filter, heater and pumps were all in working order. It was pleasing to see we didn't have any problems, so we kept the pool running for 48 hours to prove the system. Finally, we had ironed out the problems and had our first prototype. But most importantly we had a viable product that could be sold to customers.

At the outset I thought the pool was going to take us around 8 weeks to build, in the end it took us 14 weeks. We had many ups and downs throughout the build but we also learned a hell of a lot too. The trick as I've said before is to just get started. Everything will come to you as you need it.

We sacrificed our summer to work on a product to prove we had a business. I challenged myself to build the first container pool, so I could see and learn with my own head and hands how it was done. Now I'll be writing an operation manual on how to build a container pool step by step which will include a part list for a 40ft container pool build. I'll then be tasking employees to build a 20ft container pool and documenting the same information so an operation manual can also be written.

DEFINE AND GROW

Out of this chapter, here is your space to clarify your thinking, set your goals, chart the benefits, and hold yourself accountable in order to see your business and personal growth in action.

ACTION NEEDED	BENEFIT TO BUSINESS	IMPLEMENT BY (date)
1 _____	_____	__ / __ / __
_____	_____	
_____	_____	
2 _____	_____	__ / __ / __
_____	_____	
_____	_____	
3 _____	_____	__ / __ / __
_____	_____	
_____	_____	

NOTES

CHAPTER 12   PRACTICAL STEPS TO SETTING UP A BUSINESS

In this chapter we'll look at some basic steps required for setting up a company in preparation to start trading.

WHAT'S IN A NAME?

What will you call your business? Choosing a business name can be a lengthy process, but a clear, powerful name can be extremely helpful in your branding and marketing efforts.

Once you've chosen your business name, you will be able to make progress with other tasks.

My top 5 tips for finding your perfect business names are:

1. Try and devise a name for your business that will allow for growth and development. Don't simply pick a name that describes you as a bookseller, which may cause issues if at some stage you decide to develop and sell music and dvd's. Amazon is a perfect example of how their business name has allowed them to expand into other markets without them having to rebrand.

2. When trying to develop a name – think about how it sounds and how easy it is to say. Is it easy to spell and clearly heard when announcing it on the telephone to customers? Can it be abbreviated and still make sense?

3. It's helpful to think about your product or service and whether that can be incorporated into your business name. This helps to make it easily identifiable when customers are searching online. What are your

values, your passion, your motivating desires to want to run your own business in your chosen sector? There can be a whole range of ideas that pop up that will help you to come up with the business name that is right for you. Be creative – but unless you have the finances to employ a branding and marketing agency to help you push your new business and its brand name out into the public domain, it may be wise to keep things simple.

4. If you choose to involve family and friends in trying to come up with a name, try to present only the final 3 choices to a small group of people. Don't present a long list of possibilities to all and sundry, otherwise you will find that it will become impossible to make a decision. There is a saying: "a camel is a horse, designed by committee"; which basically means, do not involve too many people in trying to make a single decision or you will end up with too many conflicting opinions and a poor result.

5. Test your name out on Google AdWords. One of the great features of the "find keywords" tool on AdWords is that it will list similar search phrases, along with how many global and local monthly searches each are getting. By conducting searches on AdWords with the name you're considering you can ensure there is no conflict of interest in what you have chosen.

6. Register It. If you've decided that Limited company status is the right path for you, then you will need to register your business with Companies House. This is an easy process you can do yourself or there are companies who will do this for you, for a fee. If you have decided

to use an accountant to assist with your business set up, then this is something that they will be able to deal with on your behalf.

FINANCIALS

REGISTER AN ACCOUNTANT:

When it comes to running a business, unless you are particularly adept at doing absolutely everything, some things are best left to a professional and accounts is one such area. It may be that you are just starting out and can't afford the expense of an accountant when a simple book-keeper will do. Limited companies are very likely to benefit from using an accountant as they understand many different aspects of tax laws and can often advise on making decisions which help your business positively. For example, there may be a tax relief you can apply to your accounts to reduce the amount owed to HMRC. An accountant will know the latest rules and regulations to follow and help you apply this, which can save you money, as well as keeping you on track with year-end tax submissions.

Sole traders and Partnerships will also be required to submit self-assessment accounts in line with a schedule set down by HMRC and, again, an accountant can help you calculate this. Shop around and look at packages and rates on offer in your local area. TaxAssist Accountants are one such company that are perfect for small businesses and self-employed individuals looking to manage their financial and tax affairs on a budget.

VAT REGISTRATION

In the UK, all businesses with taxable turnover of £85,000 or more are required to be registered for VAT. There is no cost to register and you can use an accountant to complete your return, or file it yourself. You will need the following information to hand in order to register for VAT:

- National Insurance (NI) number or 'tax identifier' – a unique taxpayer's reference
- Certificate of incorporation/incorporation details
- Details of all associated businesses within the last two years
- Business bank account details
- Details of the business that has been transferred (acquired), if appropriate
- The current way to register for VAT is online only

HMRC is paperless. All newly VAT-registered businesses are required to submit their VAT returns and any VAT payments electronically.

In order to gain access to the VAT online services, you must first have registered for HMRC Online Services or the Government Gateway. Once you are all set up you can link your accounting software such as Xero to your VAT returns, which are submitted on a quarterly basis.

SETTING UP THE SUPPLY CHAIN:

This can be another time-consuming activity, but you'll find you prioritise setting up your main suppliers first and as the business grows, you will constantly add new suppliers.

As a new company it can be difficult to get credit accounts. Most suppliers will credit search the business through Creditsafe (a piece of software you should also be investing in if your customers are a B2B so you can also credit-check your customers and give them the correct credit limits).

The results from the supplier search on your business will likely give you a credit score of around 35-40 and a credit limit of £500. You may have to negotiate with suppliers to have this increased. If they are stubborn, try to set milestones you can both measure, a period of time which involves them giving you credit and you paying them back early, or sometimes upfront with a view to building the relationship quickly and them gaining your trust on paying. Some may even ask you to personally guarantee the credit.

I had this situation in the first business I ever set up. I negotiated a deal with my main supplier to buy 60% of our products through them. The first order was a Pro-forma invoice that meant paying up front. Then they gave us £1 thousand credit which was paid on time every month with a view to increasing our credit limit every month by £1k if we did pay on time. Over the next 12 months we had built up a credit limit of 12k. When we were setting up with other suppliers, they would only give us a limit of £500 because the computer said "no". So, this approach can work to build a good credit relationship with a supplier.

It's very difficult in the beginning to get credit as your cash flow is so tight, but there are strategies to assist you to be able to make it work. You may have to look at how you charge your customers to help fund projects or to gain stock, depending what your business does.

The benefit of having more suppliers does give you the opportunity to get the best prices by comparing them against one and other. I would always get 3 different quotes from each supplier to get a best price before placing an order. Again, this takes time because it's usually the suppliers that delay the process because you find you are constantly waiting for them to come back to you with their best price. Being patient here is key as it can save you money depending on the size of the order being placed.

DEFINE AND GROW

Out of this chapter, here is your space to clarify your thinking, set your goals, chart the benefits, and hold yourself accountable in order to see your business and personal growth in action.

ACTION NEEDED	BENEFIT TO BUSINESS	IMPLEMENT BY (date)
1 _____	_____	__ / __ / __
_____	_____	
_____	_____	
2 _____	_____	__ / __ / __
_____	_____	
_____	_____	
3 _____	_____	__ / __ / __
_____	_____	
_____	_____	

NOTES

CHAPTER 13   AN ONLINE PRESENCE

INTERNET MARKETING

Once you've chosen your company name, the next step is to secure the domain name for your website and email address. If possible, secure the .co.uk (if you are in the UK) and .com domain name rather than alternatives such as .net, .org, .biz, or other possible domain extensions.

A quick check to see if the domain name is available can be done on sites such as GoDaddy.com or NetworkSolutions.com. If the domain name is taken you may be able to track down the owner of the domain name and see if they are willing to sell it. However, if you can avoid this in the first instance by choosing an alternative name, that would be preferable.

If your business is based in the UK, I would also look at purchasing the co.uk as this will stop any competition purchasing just so they can be on the same Google page as you and potentially steel customers. If social media is going to play a part in your marketing strategy, remember to also open accounts on popular sites such as Facebook, Twitter, Instagram and Pinterest.

CREATING YOUR WEBSITE

Your website is an online catalogue and shop window open 24/7 of your product and service offerings, for new and potential customers. Your website needs to be visually appealing to customers whilst structured to carry out good effective marketing.

Below is a brief guide to six essential stages to creating a successful website.

1. Like many businesses, you may choose to utilise the services of an experienced web designer to create your site. This will begin with 'information gathering' in which the web team will gather

information from you to learn what you do and don't want your site to do. It is helpful if you are able to research other sites you currently use, along with your competitors sites. Be prepared to answer questions from the web team as the answers will help to produce a creative brief that the designers will work from.

Regardless of whether you use a design firm or not, it is helpful if you can answer the following questions:

- What is the purpose of my site? Am I providing a service, a product, information, or collecting data?
- What action do I want my visitors to take upon visiting the site?
- Who am I trying to reach? What are the demographics of my audience?
- What kind of information will my target audience be looking for? Are they looking for specific information, a particular product, online ordering?

If you can answer these questions with honesty and clarity then you'll know the purpose, the goals, target audience and content of your website. These are basic questions any good web designer will ask you. Be prepared to go into more detail so the designer has the best understanding of exactly what you want to achieve.

2. Next steps are to look at creating a site map and the designers should produce this. It is basically a list of all main topic areas of the site, as well as sub-topics. This helps to develop a consistent, easy to understand navigational system. As use of mobile devices continues to increase, the designers will take into account how your website is displayed across a desktop, tablet or smartphone.

The web designers will obviously require content for your website and you should be either able to produce this yourself (to keep costs down) or they can provide a copy writer to write your content or edit your content for you. Again this is something to discuss with the designers and agree on costs. It's no good having a beautifully designed visual website if the copy is not up to scratch.

3. Again, if you're using a web designer, they will help with these next steps. If you're attempting to do this yourself, then in order to get the home page (and subsequent pages) design and function correct, you will need to know what the demographic of your target audience is, ie. are they single, female, middle-class, ages 18 to 24, and college educated versus married, male, upper class, ages 65 to 80, and retired? Knowing all of this definitely affects what design elements and applications to use.

Seeing page layouts with real content and photos, along with your logo and colours will really bring your vision of the site to life. Use this time to make necessary changes. If you're working with experienced designers, they will provide mock-ups or prototypes in several developmental stages for feedback. Making changes is costly and more difficult to implement later.

4. Once the design work is done and approved, the website can be created. Your designer/developer will take all the individual graphic elements from the prototype and use them to create a functional site. Interactive elements like contact forms, animations and shopping carts will be implemented in this phase too. During this time, you'll still be able to make minor changes and corrections.

5. Time to test, deliver and launch! Your web developer will test your website, from complete functionality to compatibility issues. Additionally, the developer will check to be sure that all of the code written for your website validates - meeting current web standards. Once final approval is given, website files will be uploaded to your servers, and then the site will be pushed live to the public.

6. Now that it's finally built, it's equally as important to maintain your site. During the planning stage of this process, you should have already determined whether or not you would keep the maintenance in-house or outsource to a third party (like your web designer). If you decided you needed full control, the designer would have designed a site driven by a CMS to give you the ability to edit content areas of your site as well as add new pages.

DEFINE AND GROW

Out of this chapter, here is your space to clarify your thinking, set your goals, chart the benefits, and hold yourself accountable in order to see your business and personal growth in action.

ACTION NEEDED	BENEFIT TO BUSINESS	IMPLEMENT BY (date)
1 _____	_____	__ / __ / __
_____	_____	
_____	_____	
2 _____	_____	__ / __ / __
_____	_____	
_____	_____	
3 _____	_____	__ / __ / __
_____	_____	
_____	_____	

NOTES

CHAPTER 14   WHOEVER SAID IT WOULD BE EASY?

Time is the only commodity money can't buy and we certainly can't get it back. Choosing how you spend your time and making the most of your time is a most important decision to make.

There are going to be days where you don't want to show up because you are under pressure and these will be tough times which are sent to test us and shape who we are and who we become. Embrace these types of days/weeks or even months because in time when you reflect on how far you've come, you will see how this has made you and your businesses reach new heights.

My advice is blunt, simple and effective if executed. Get up and show up every day. You have to lead by example. If you don't do it, who will? After all, this is your business and you're responsible for the results it produces. You're responsible for being the leader of your business. You're the one everyone else is looking up to.

Looking back on experiences, I wanted to share this particular one here because it's one that happened to me in the very beginning. Yes, I was fresh (but completely out of my depth) because I had only just started my business. But on the other hand, I was diving straight in the deep, so to speak, and I had two choices. Sink or swim.

I had worked very hard to secure a large contract for the design and build of a new health and fitness country club in Cheshire. Our scope of works was the design and installation of the filtration systems on 2 indoor swimming pools, one outdoor swimming, one outdoor spa pool and a wellness pool. As I've mentioned, talk about jumping in at the deep end!

Bearing in mind, here I was, a one-man band - I was the only employee. I had done my salesman spiel and negotiated and secured the project. My next role was to design the pools with the help of an AutoCAD specialist who could produce the necessary drawings, along with my experienced input with regards to pipe work sizes, routes, plant and equipment.

Shortly after we finished the design it was time to start on-site where my role was to change to installation engineer and project manager, procuring materials to install. From start to finish I installed the project with my own two hands and a lot of late nights and weekend working.

In-between this time I was also running the business, answering enquiries diverted to my mobile phone, book-keeping and everything else needed to keep the business going. I was living proof of a typical start-up business with the owner wearing the many different hats and juggling his roles.

The site installation work took me around 6 months to carry out and as the project came to an end and we filled and commissioned each pool, I walked around the build and my thoughts were; "I have designed this and I have installed this". A huge sense of achievement came over me.

At this point I had been installing pools for 16 years, but it was always for somebody else and always with a team of people to help me. Something like this gives you confidence and also shifts any self-limiting beliefs you may have when you wonder; can I stand on my own two feet?

My answer was an overwhelming yes. The reason I wanted to add this story is because as I write this, we have just secured the same project from the same client who is building their second country club. Only, this time around, the role will be a whole lot different for me - which shows the growth and the structure I now have in place from when we did the first project several years ago.

You see, for every role I had to do back then; I now have a structured team of employees in every position to carry out this project with very little physical input from me. That is progression, and all as a result from everything that has been implemented by me that you have read throughout this book. The timeframe from back then to now, to get to this stage took 6 years. Seems more like 6 minutes because time flies when you're having fun, right?!

I'm not going to lie; these were tough times and a very steep learning curve. I had created a job not a business, as at the time as I was doing all the roles which needed 5-6 employees. I knew this wasn't sustainable but something I just had to get on with.

In the end, all the hard work paid off for both me and also my client. The club became a huge success and I was well underway to being able to pour back in the funds I had made from that project to start building a sustainable company.

On reflection there are some takeaway learning observations here: -

1. It required sacrifice and determination to deliver that project by me.
2. Working in multiple roles within the business at the beginning.
3. Gaining vital experience in every role prepared me for the staff I needed for growth.
4. I learned that anything is possible if you put your mind to it.
5. Business is a process and doesn't just happen overnight. There are crucial incremental steps and milestones that have to be achieved until the day it all slots into place.
6. Fake it till you make it works, if you have the desire and hunger to deliver on your promises.

And as Hannibal from the great TV show the A team used to say. . . "I love it when a plan comes together."

So, it's good to remember when you're going through the tough times that there is light at the other end of the tunnel and when you see that light you'll then have all the 'nay-sayers' saying things like, "Oh it's alright for you", blah blah blah. . . because they weren't there in the beginning when you were going through the difficulties and challenges business throws at you.

But at least by then you'll just be able to smile and think to yourself. . . if only you knew.

ADVICE WITH VALUE

1. Get up and show up everyday
2. Embrace the tough times
3. I love it when a plan comes together

DEFINE AND GROW

Out of this chapter, here is your space to clarify your thinking, set your goals, chart the benefits, and hold yourself accountable in order to see your business and personal growth in action.

ACTION NEEDED	BENEFIT TO BUSINESS	IMPLEMENT BY (date)
1		__ / __ / __
2		__ / __ / __
3		__ / __ / __

NOTES

CHAPTER 15   THE WAY OUT

SELF-REMOVAL

A way out from your business may not be in the forefront of your mind when you're first setting out. It sounds strange that we would plan to leave the very business we are about to grow and develop. It's worth remembering though, that there may well come a time that your business will run better without you. You may be staring at this page and thinking "I don't think so", but it will, trust me. Sure, there's a lot to do before you get to this stage, but if you have a plan right from the start then it allows you to build a successful company with you working *on* the business rather than in *it*, on a day to day basis.

In order to achieve your own self-removal, you will need to pay attention to the fundamental principles I have outlined in this book; setting up systems, employing great people, marketing strategies, coaching/mentoring/self-development and understanding finances.

All of these principles are so important to help scale any successful business, and by now you should have identified through your vision and your goals whether your business is being built to sell, or are your intentions to pass it down to family members to run?

As you are at this stage of the book, I'd like to recommend a must-read book; 'Built to Sell' by John Warrilow. The clue is in the title and it is an easy read with plenty of information to execute your growing business. This book in particular has helped me develop my businesses. I read this book once a year and every time I read it, something new resonates with me as I progress through my business journey.

At some point, but mostly at the start-up phase, everyone becomes attached to their business. Some may even call their business, their baby. This is where we have to change our thinking. Your business is a vehicle to financial freedom. That is how we should look and think about it. Yes, be passionate about what you do, but do not wrap your arms around it and cherish it like it was your first born. We have to learn to let go and trust others with the vehicle. The business cannot, and should not, be built around you. It has to be built around others. Selecting others can be very challenging in itself and you will not get it right all the time, you may even have to kiss a few frogs to find your prince. Be persistent here and your hard work will pay off long term.

DEFINE AND GROW

Out of this chapter, here is your space to clarify your thinking, set your goals, chart the benefits, and hold yourself accountable in order to see your business and personal growth in action.

ACTION NEEDED	BENEFIT TO BUSINESS	IMPLEMENT BY (date)
① _____	_____	__ / __ / __
_____	_____	
_____	_____	
② _____	_____	__ / __ / __
_____	_____	
_____	_____	
③ _____	_____	__ / __ / __
_____	_____	
_____	_____	

NOTES

WHO IS THE AUTHOR, DEAN THISTLETON?

Dean grew up on a council estate in Manchester, UK, with his mother and older brother. Times were tough and a real struggle most of the time. What he did know, from an early age, is that he desired a better quality of life for his own future. Coming from these humble beginnings however, Dean was also taught the foundational value of working to earn. This is a path he chose early on, and at thirteen years old his persistence paid off by finding someone to employ him at such a young age. He worked on a milk delivery round.

"I was very thankful for the opportunity that was given to me, even though it meant I was getting up at 4am, four days a week. Having the milk round gave me my first taste of earning money. And I liked it. The job was doing two things for me at the time. It was paying me money, and it was also keeping me off the streets at night due to the early starts."

"Working from an early age gave me the work ethic that I have today. I guess you can say that it has become a habit that has been ingrained in me from the such a young age," says Dean. "We all have choices in life and back then I made a decision to work hard and stay off the streets, unlike some of my friends I grew up with in my community who found out the hard way by being on the wrong side of the law."

Dean learned much from the milk round owner, who had an exemplary work ethic which he passed on to Dean, probably without him even knowing it. Over the years, the milk round work grew into tiling work on weekends with the same person.

"I left school with some basic qualifications, nothing to write home about, really. Being from a council estate the expectation wasn't really high for good grades. But what I did gain in these years was a strong work ethic. I didn't have A's or B's to brag about, but I knew I wanted to work hard and earn as much money as I could." This set Dean on a purposeful course that eventually led him, through good timing, thoughtful serendipity, and the Law of Attraction, to work for a swimming pool company.

"I went for the interview and one question that I will always remember being asked, was: 'Where do you see yourself in five years?' And I said to the director, opposite, who was interviewing me, 'Sitting where you are, in your position.' That raised a smile from him, but I was serious." And I got the job.

By now, Dean had just turned seventeen and was excited to be starting a new challenge, and learning something new from scratch. Weekend working was constantly being asked for, and he happily obliged. This was nothing new to Dean as he had been doing it for four years already, by this time.

"There were other apprentices who had started before me, and when I bumped into them on occasions at the office they would ask me why I kept working on weekends. And I told them, 'So that I can learn faster.' And learn faster he did.

Within six months Dean was promoted to semi-skilled engineer, and then after another three months he was promoted again to skilled engineer, just before his eighteenth birthday. "I was the youngest engineer, and was also the quickest to become a skilled engineer in our industry. Something I will be forever proud of."

He was on a mission to become the best engineer within the company and also to make it through the ranks to become director. For Dean, coming through the ranks is important, so that one can learn the skills of the trade, and experience many of the positions you would be overseeing as a director. Dean spent eight years working as a swimming pool engineer, working on some high-profile projects – not making it into that particular director's chair in that specific company. However, he was head-hunted by another swimming pool company, and was soon running several big projects and meeting deadlines and budgets for these. Within a short space of time, Dean was promoted to on-site project manager, all the time gaining knowledge and a skill-set that he knew would help him when setting up his own businesses in the future.

This time wasn't far in the making. "I had been working alongside my current boss for nearly seven years. I will always remember him saying to me at the start: 'Learn as much knowledge as you can from me while I'm still around.' That I did in abundance. He was a role model to me and I would be happy with my own share measured against the success of his life. He was a multi-millionaire through many businesses, but the main cash cow was the swimming pool business. Modelling successful people is a very good trait to have and it certainly worked for me," says Dean.

By the age of 31, Dean had already had two pivotal role models in life, with both of them being former bosses. "I was ready, ready to go it alone and set up my own business." His boss was very understanding, and said that he knew this time would come, so it wasn't a shock to him. If anything, he was prepared, and, 'to be honest, I already knew he would be,' says Dean.

Dean had the boss's blessing, along with his help to get established. However, he also told Dean that before he made his final decision to go it alone then and there, that he had a contract on his desk, ready to sign, to build the London 2012 Olympic pools – but that he wouldn't, and couldn't, do it without Dean on board. "I knew that committing to this project would tie me in for at least two years. But jobs in our industry didn't come more prestigious than this, and I also knew that it would do wonders for my CV," Dean added. "I didn't feel like I was putting life on hold for one minute. I looked at the bigger picture for the future. I knew that delivering this project would elevate me and, in turn, my new company." So Dean committed to this esteemed once-in-a-lifetime project.

At the same time, Dean set about doing some groundwork for his new company, registering it and setting up supplier accounts, ready to start trade. "Delivering the Olympic pools in London was a great achievement and something I will be forever proud of. However, I promised myself that someday I will deliver as big a project as the Olympic pools again, but this time with my own company."

In 2012, the doors were officially opened for Dean's first business, Concept Pools. He had confidence and energy to make this company a success, which it continues to be today, alongside other businesses too, reaching multi-million turnover.

A final word for now from Dean: "I hope that you can take inspiration and implement some of the strategies I have learned and implemented to build a company from Scratch to a million-pound turnover business."

As Dean's business grows, his intention is to bring new insights into what it takes to make your first million (Scratch to a Million – this book), what can be learned from making £3–5 million, £5–10 million. Enjoy the journey of his, and your, success with Dean Thistleton, determined entrepreneur.